For Paul —L. F. M.

The publisher and author gratefully acknowledge the expert review
of this book by Deborah Epperson, Ph.D.

Published by National Geographic Partners, LLC, Washington, DC 20036.

Book design by YAY! Design

Trade paperback ISBN: 978-1-4263-1472-8
Reinforced library binding ISBN: 978-1-4263-1473-5

Table of Contents

Who Am I?

I have whiskers,
but I am not a cat.

I nibble on grass,
but I am not a cow.

I have gray, wrinkled
skin, but I am not an
elephant.

Who am I?
A manatee!

Mighty Manatees

Manatees often rest in groups.

Manatees are mammals that live in the water. They are sometimes called "sea cows."

Why?

Manatees are gentle and they move slowly, like cows. They also graze on sea grass, just like cows eat grass.

Water Words

MAMMAL: An animal that has a backbone and is warm-blooded. It feeds its babies milk.

GRAZE: To feed in an area covered with grasses

Manatees are big. They are usually about ten feet long. That's as long as two kids' bikes lined up end to end.

Manatees are heavy, too.
Most adult manatees weigh about
1,000 pounds. That's the weight
of about 21 second graders!

Super Swimmers

Manatees can move their large bodies gracefully through the water. They swim upside down and roll. They even do somersaults (SUM-ur-sawlts)!

A group of manatees swims in Crystal River, Florida, U.S.A.

Manatees don't like water that is too deep. They like to stay in shallow water in oceans and rivers. There, they find food and warm water.

A manatee's body
is built for living in
the water.

TAIL: It is large, flat, and round at the end. It moves up and down to power the manatee through the water.

EYES: They are small, but manatees can see well, even in cloudy water.

NOSTRILS: Manatees breathe air through these holes. But they close tightly underwater.

FLIPPERS: They help steer the manatee. They also bring food to its mouth.

LIPS: They are big and strong. They wrap around plants and pull them into the manatee's mouth.

13

Munching on Lunch

Manatees are herbivores (HUR-buh-vores). They eat plants for about six to eight hours every day.

A manatee grazes on sea plants.

Manatees have no front teeth. They don't need them because they don't eat meat.

Manatees have only large back teeth called molars. The molars help grind their food.

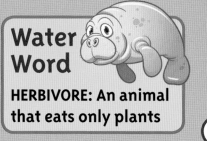

Water Word

HERBIVORE: An animal that eats only plants

7 Fun Facts About Manatees

1 They lose teeth all through their lives. New teeth replace them.

2 The elephant is a distant relative of the manatee.

3 Fat in the mother's milk helps a young manatee grow quickly.

4

They do not have eyelashes.

5

human

manatee

Bones in a manatee's flipper are similar to those in a human hand.

6

They do not use their mouth to breathe. They only use their nostrils.

7

They have no natural enemies. Humans are their biggest threat.

Big Babies

These young manatees are fed milk from a bottle.
Without their mothers, they need help to eat.

A manatee baby is called a calf.
It is born underwater. A newborn
calf is about the size of a nine-
year-old kid.

The mother pushes the calf to
the surface to take its first breath.
Within an hour, the calf can
swim on its own.

Like other mammal babies, a manatee drinks its mother's milk. Soon it learns how to find sea grasses to eat.

A calf needs to stick with its mom.

The calf must stay with its mother for the first two years. The mother teaches her calf how to live on its own.

On the Move

Manatees do not stay in one place. They migrate (MY-grate).

In summer, manatees can be found in many states. In winter, most manatees return to Florida. The water is warmer there.

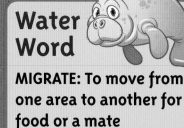

Water Word

MIGRATE: To move from one area to another for food or a mate

MILES
0   200   400

KILOMETERS
0   200   400

C A N A D A

U N I T E D

S T A T E S

MISSISSIPPI

LOUISIANA

ALABAMA

GEORGIA

VIRGINIA

MARYLAND

Chesapeake Bay

NORTH CAROLINA

SOUTH
CAROLINA

FLORIDA

Florida Keys

Straits of Florida

A T L A N T I C   O C E A N

B A H A M A S

GULF OF MEXICO

90°   80°   70°

Area where Florida manatees
live year-round

Area where Florida manatees
travel in summer

Manatees at Rest

Manatees don't usually travel in groups. But they often rest together in warm water.

Manatees need rest, like you. But they don't sleep like you do.

They rest for about 15 minutes at a time. Then they need to come to the surface to breathe.

Manatees sometimes rest at the bottom of the sea or river. They can also float near the top of the water when resting.

Keeping Manatees Safe

There are many dangers for manatees. They are often hit by boats because they are big and slow and swim near the surface. Manatees can be hard to see in the water.

Manatee Zone
SLOW SPEED
MINIMUM WAKE
Sep 1 - Apr 30
35 MPH Day 25MPH Night
May 1 - Aug 31

This manatee has scars from an injury by a boat propeller.

People also throw trash and fishing line into the water. Swallowing trash can hurt manatees. Fishing line can get tangled around manatees so they can't swim.

Manatees are endangered
(in-DANE-jurd).
There are about 5,000
Florida manatees left.

But laws protect them.
There are also special
areas for manatees called
sanctuaries (SANGK-choo-
er-eez). In a sanctuary,
people can't disturb
manatees. They can live
safely there and raise
their young.

The roped-off area shows where people are not allowed to go.

Water
Word

ENDANGERED: At risk of
dying out

SANCTUARY: A safe place
set aside for animals in
nature

Stump Your Parents

Can your parents answer these questions about manatees? You might know more than they do!

Answers at bottom of page 31.

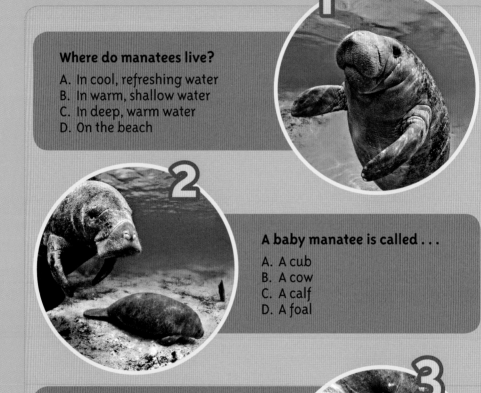

Where do manatees live?

A. In cool, refreshing water
B. In warm, shallow water
C. In deep, warm water
D. On the beach

A baby manatee is called . . .

A. A cub
B. A cow
C. A calf
D. A foal

What do manatees like to eat?

A. Plants
B. Crabs
C. Fruit
D. Steak

4

A manatee's lips . . .

A. Are very small
B. Are perfect for lipstick
C. Get in the way when eating
D. Grab and pull plants into its mouth

5

Manatees rest . . .

A. For many hours
B. For about 30 minutes at a time
C. For about 15 minutes at a time
D. Not at all

6

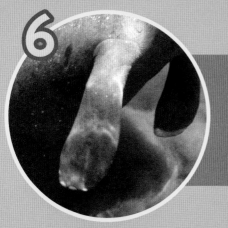

A manatee uses its flippers to . . .

A. Do the backstroke
B. Slap the water
C. Steer through the water
D. Wave to other manatees

7

To keep manatees safe, people should NOT . . .

A. Bother manatees in any way
B. Drive boats really fast
C. Throw trash in the water
D. Do any of the above

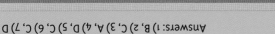

Answers: 1) B, 2) C, 3) A, 4) D, 5) C, 6) C, 7) D

ENDANGERED: At risk of dying out

GRAZE: To feed in an area covered with grasses

HERBIVORE: An animal that eats only plants

MAMMAL: An animal that has a backbone and is warm-blooded. It feeds its babies milk.

MIGRATE: To move from one area to another for food or a mate

SANCTUARY: A safe place set aside for animals in nature

Sea Turtles

Laura Marsh

NATIONAL
GEOGRAPHIC

Washington, D.C.